Politics, Prophesy, and The Pillage of the Church

POLITICS, PROPHESY, AND THE PILLAGE OF THE CHURCH

Niyi Olusoji, EdD

XULON PRESS

Xulon Press
2301 Lucien Way #415
Maitland, FL 32751
407.339.4217
www.xulonpress.com

© 2022 by Niyi Olusoji, EdD

All rights reserved solely by the author. The author guarantees all contents are original and do not infringe upon the legal rights of any other person or work. No part of this book may be reproduced in any form without the permission of the author.

Due to the changing nature of the Internet, if there are any web addresses, links, or URLs included in this manuscript, these may have been altered and may no longer be accessible. The views and opinions shared in this book belong solely to the author and do not necessarily reflect those of the publisher. The publisher therefore disclaims responsibility for the views or opinions expressed within the work.

Unless otherwise indicated, Scripture quotations taken from the New King James Version (NKJV). Copyright © 1982 by Thomas Nelson, Inc. Used by permission. All rights reserved.

Paperback ISBN-13: 978-1-6628-4417-1
Ebook ISBN-13: 978-1-6628-4418-8

Acknowledgment

This book is a culmination of thoughts about the Christian religion and the characteristics of individuals referred to as Christians. The inspiration for this writing came from my Christian experience under the tutelage of steadfast men and women of God. These are individuals who God used to save my life and keep my feet on the path of righteousness. I also cherish the brotherly love that I enjoyed from those men and women I worked with over many years in the vineyard of the Lord. These relationships and experiences gave me an idea about Christian growth, and the knowledge gained is responsible for the Christian culture that I have come to love and cherish. To these individuals too numerous to mention, I owe you gratitude for accepting me the way I am and helping me develop my Christian ideals. Finally, I want to thank my wife and children for their spiritual and moral support at all times. This little contribution to Christian literature is dedicated to the Almighty God, the Fountain of Knowledge and Hope.

List of Contents

Acknowledgment vii
Preface xiii
Introduction xv

Part I

The Bible 1
    The God of the Bible 2
    The World 3
    The Christian World 4
    Biblical Worldview 5
    Christian Growth 8
    Implications of Christian Growth to Worldview 12

Part II

Christianity And Prophecy 15
    The Doctrine of Prophecy 17
    The Prophet 18
    Prophets and Prophecy 19
    Prophecy And Other Doctrines 20
    Sources of Prophecy 23

Part III

A True Prophet 27
    Analysis from the Definition 28
    True Prophecy 29
    Prophetic Revelations 30
    Prophetic Utterances 31
    Fulfilled Prophecies 33
    Unfulfilled Prophecies 34
    Timing and Prophecy 35
    God's Intervention in the Affairs of Men........... 37
    The Call to Be a Prophet 38
    The Modern-Day Prophets....................... 40

Part IV

The Human Experience 43
    Experience from a Global Perspective.............. 45
    When Prophecy Goes Awry 47
    A Prophetic Case Study 49
    When Only the Best Matters 51
    Prophet's Incursion into Politics 52
    Prophets and National Politics.................... 53
    The Church and Politics......................... 54

Part V

The Assault on the Church.......................... 57
    How Did We Get Here?......................... 58
    Putting Things in the Right Perspective............. 60
    Where Do We Go from Here? 61

List of Contents

What Do We Hope to Achieve? 62
How Do We Begin? 63
Back to Our Root 65
Focusing on the Bible 67

Part VI

God Will Work Out His Plan 69
   God Is the Ultimate 70
   On a Personal Note 70
   The Presidential Prophecy 72
   Relationship of the Prophecy with the Present Situation . 74
   A Biblical Example 76
   Relationship of the Prophesy to End Time Events 78
   A Word for Christian Leaders. 79
   The Conclusion 81

Preface

The church of God is going through a turbulent time, but the believer's hope should rest on the solace of the words of our Savior written in the book of Mathew chapter 16 verse 18 that He will build His church and that the gates of hell shall not prevail against it. The idea that God will build the church and protect the same bestowed a responsibility upon the leadership and members of the church. They must be seen to be working at building the church and protecting it under the empowerment of the Lord, the Master Builder. The Lord needs the hands of Christians in the building process, but it appears that the church is concerned with mundane things of this world. Christians have become lovers of the world and not lovers of the Lord. The church is under severe attack, and it has been fragmented along cultural lines of gender, politics, and many more. During the last presidential election in America, the evil one was allowed entrance into the Christian fold and, in the process, pillaged the church. This incident is not the first time that the devil will try to destroy the unity of the church. He has done it before, and he will attempt to do it again. This book tried to identify why the church has forsaken its primary roles and neglected its responsibilities. The book also tried to identify the reasons for behaviors that are not characteristics of believers. It further explains the danger of sweeping this problem under the carpet, and finally, it suggests how to heal the church so that it can move on to the performance of its divinely assigned roles.

Introduction

The inspiration for this treatise came from reviewing the role of prophets and their prophecies during the last presidential election in the USA. The election was conducted like any other election, but the umpire declared a winner that the opposition party was not expected to win. This practice is not new because every political party is working toward victory at the polls. The utterances of some prophets inflamed the controversy surrounding the election with predictions that God had chosen the loser of the election to be the winner and lead the country for another four years. Therefore, the loss at the election was seen as fraudulent, and the believers in this prophecy concluded that the declared winner had rigged the election. Their next line of action was to find another way of actualizing their dreams, and their efforts nearly turned the nation upside down. The imbroglio involved every resident of the country and many other nations that are admirers of the American democratic system of government. The Christians living within and outside America were involved in the melee.

Before the election, Christians were divided into two groups; the believers of the prophecy and those who did not believe in the prophecy. The unity of the church of God was tested, and it became compromised because of this development. The situation generated a lot of rancor before and after the election; thus, the church now has the duty of putting its house in order by uniting the dissenting factions. It was evident that something was wrong with either the prophecy or its interpretation, and the church now has a new role of explaining to the people what was wrong with the prediction. The controversy was not only between church members and family members. It was also between pastors and some church members. The controversy generated by this phenomenon was not limited to the country alone. There were a recorded number of sympathizers worldwide. It came to a level whereby Christians worldwide were encouraged to pray for one candidate over the other. This book will attempt to explain this prophecy and why prophecies may fail to materialize as expected.

This incident is not the only example where prophecy has gained notoriety. For example, many prophets in the past have prophesied the end of the world, and their predictions have failed to materialize. Recently and before the election prophecy, numerous incidences of out-of-life experiences were recorded whereby the individuals concerned reported visitations to heaven and hell after encountering the Risen Lord. Many of those involved in the encounters reported having received messages from God concerning the sinfulness of the world and the need for repentance. The issues of dreams and visions are not new, and many incidences of this nature were recorded in the Bible. Warnings about the sinfulness of the world and the punishment for sin are equally not new either.

Many prophets have preached about these topics as recorded in the Bible. Thank God that few ministers of God still preach

Introduction

about the same today. However, every believer must exercise caution because these reported incidences were mere dreams and visions and not reality. Every dream, vision, and prophetic utterance must be considered in line with the written Word, the Bible. Also, these individuals should realize that mentioning the names of individuals, whether living or dead, in their prophecies without the individual's or their representative's consent is unethical. The dead should be left alone in the hands of their Maker, while believers' efforts should be geared toward evangelizing the living who are lost.

Prophecy is a unique gift of God to humanity. It is a medium of communication between God (the Supreme Being) and His children. It serves the purpose of warning people of what is to come so they can prepare for the unexpected (something different from the normal). It also exposes the people to the reality of the moment and eases fears and anxieties from the unknown. It serves to increase the faith of believers, thereby making people move closer to God, repent from doing wrong, and have a reverent fear for God. Believers in prophecy need to have average knowledge about prophecy and the interpretation of the same. Prophecy is essential because it warns believers about the danger ahead; thus, the Bible declares that without knowing what is to come, the people are exposed to their doom (Prov. 29:18). Despite the importance of prophecies, the Bible warns about believing in prophecies without understanding what they mean and from where they emanated. Thus, we are advised to test prophecies (1 Thess. 5:20-21) because there are false prophets (Deut. 18:20-22; Matt. 7:15).

Anticipating prophecy, receiving prophecy, interpreting prophecy, testing prophecy, and applying prophecy are essential tools in making conscious and perfect use of prophecy. Most people believe in prophecy in one form or another, but few individuals make proper use of the benefits of the doctrine. Religious people request and receive prophecies from their leaders, while others look for prophecy by visiting religious cults or fortune-tellers. Many believers of prophecy focus their attention on the "who" instead of the "what." But focusing our attention on the prophet will make us revere the prophet, "who," as a god, while concentrating on the prophecy, "what," will direct us to the omnipotence of God. Therefore, making proper use of prophecy requires some degree of spiritual maturity. Relying on God is beneficial because we will gladly accept what comes our way when we submit everything to His will. We will understand why He acted in a manner, and everything will work together for our good. But when we rely solely on the prophet, we may turn him into an object of worship, and our belief in him can be fraudulently exploited.

 This book was also written to address some of the deeper meanings of Christianity as it defines a mature Christian and what is expected of the individual who is mature but still growing. Growth in Christianity is a continuous process, and Christians do not reach full maturity until they breathe their last breath. In line with Christian growth or in describing a mature Christian, the book also makes mention of attitudes and behaviors that are expected of a mature Christian. Thus, the book uses the opportunity to address the issue of spiritual maturity that qualifies an individual for spiritual leadership that will promote a Christian culture in a secular society. The roles of a mature Christian in a perplexed society are equally explored, while the book ventures exclusively on the subject of prophecy. The book tries to explain the relationship between the inhabitants of society and their beliefs and how a Christian can be easily carried away by the events in his environment. Finally, the book explores the subject of prophecy as it affects Christians and the way they are expected to view and react to the issue when they come in contact with members of other faiths.

Part I

The Bible

The position of this book is based on a biblical worldview, and all scriptural references shall be taken from the Christian's Holy Bible. The Bible is the holy book for the adherents of the Christian religion. Christianity began as the offshoot of Judaism. The Judaism book of Law (Torah), in combination with other writings, especially those known as the book of the prophets, formed the Old Testament of the Bible. The books that contain the history of the life and ministry of our Lord Jesus Christ and early Christianity are called the New Testament. The combination of the Old and the New Testament is called the Holy Bible. The entire Bible is a history book, a record book, and a book for instruction in righteousness or Christian living. The writing of the Bible followed the inspiration of God; hence it is termed the Word of God (2 Peter 1:21). Some Bible passages also support the direct command of God to the prophets to write down His messages or instructions. Examples of these can be found in Exodus 17:14, Exodus 34:27, Jeremiah 30:2, Habakkuk 2:2, and Revelation 1:19.

Other authors of the books of the Bible wrote as they were moved by the Holy Spirit. Like any other book that was written by inspiration, Bible authors were inspired by the Holy Spirit who dwelled in them. The Christian is expected to study the Bible, meditate on the words of the Bible, and learn from studying the Bible and from the teachings and life of Bible teachers and elders. Also, Christians are expected to pray regularly and follow the directives in the Bible. They are to allow these practices to form the foundation of their lives, termed the work and the walk of a Christian. Thus, the Christian sees or perceives the world differently from his non-Christian neighbor, even though they live in the same worldly environment. Christians live like any other individual but have at the back of their mind that they are different individuals with the liberty to do all things, but who have limitations as written in the Bible. Thus, the Christian will not just do anything, go everywhere, and be anything. Whenever the Christian performs an action or exhibits a behavior, it is expected to be without sin and with moderation.

The God of the Bible

We cannot talk about any Bible theme without referring to the God of the Bible, Who also is the author of the Bible. Every tribal group or culture has a concept of God or a Supreme Being in one form or another. The God of the Bible is the One who revealed Himself to humanity through His chosen people, the Israelites. He also made Himself known to different tribal groups scattered all over the world through His chosen people. Thus, the conception of God became a true manifestation as individuals began to speak to Him and hear Him speak to them. He manifested His power through the deliverance of His people and the destruction of those who attempted to stand in His way. Even though His numerous attributes surround us, many do not know Him. He revealed Himself in the Bible as the Angel of the Lord in the Old Testament and as Jesus Christ the Messiah in the New Testament. His presence still surrounds us today as always in the person of the Holy Spirit. In all these manifestations, He never relinquished His throne in heaven. Because of this attribute, He is referred to as the Trinity as He presents Himself as God the Father, God the Son, and God the Holy Spirit. God the Father is a Spirit, God the Holy Spirit is a Spirit, and God the Son is a Spirit who took human form when He became the Savior; thus, He is the only familiar face that we will see in heaven as our Advocate. This synopsis is a valid gospel message, and this is why we are compelled to preach Him to the whole world.

The World

The world means the environment where we live and the social interactions between us and the environment that determines the way we live. As social beings, young humans begin learning from their nuclear families and later learn from the society where they are domiciled. Humans influence society, and society equally influences the inhabitants; thus, humans' behaviors can be peculiar to the environment where they live. In the fallen world where we find ourselves, we tend to do what is socially acceptable and prefer not to be seen as outcasts or antisocial. Most of the behaviors exhibited in our society are against biblical injunctions, and they are hated by God, Who gave the directive that we should abstain from them. These behaviors are termed sins, and we are encouraged to abstain from them for our benefit. For example, a man who commits adultery may invoke the wrath of his wife, and the cost may be unbearable. This type of behavior is against the will of God that we should love one another because the adulterer does not love his wife or his neighbor. Humanity's display of this type of attitude is why God decided to punish sinners. A non-adherent of the Christian faith may be living in sin or not know that he is not living right. Some might even argue against instructions, but those humble enough to learn the history of the human race, especially the fall of man, will realize that sin is a frequent occurrence in our daily lives.

The Christian World

The Christian world is not a different planet from the world of non-Christians. It is the same world with differing perspectives. While the average individual sees the world as a place where everything goes, the Christian views this world as a condemned world. According to the Bible, it is a condemned world because our world is full of sin, and the repercussion for this sinfulness is death and destruction. Historically, the world at the time of Adam and Eve has been described as a destroyed world because God destroyed the earth due to men's sinfulness. The present world is described as a condemned world because of our sins and the plan of Christ to bring vengeance to the world by the time of His second coming. The world to come (a new world or new earth) that will be free from sin is the view that shapes the Christian's perspective. Jesus ascertained in one of His speeches that believers are in the world but not of the world (John 17:14). Believers see Christianity as a way of life, and Christians are expected to live according to the dictates of the Bible. They are expected to live at peace with their neighbors (Rom. 12:18) and run away from all appearances of evil (1 Thess. 5:22), popularly known as sin.

Many religious faiths and religious books also contain statutes on sins or wrongdoings and righteousness or good behaviors. They also teach and believe in the art of prophecy. However, our direction for this book will be taken from the Christian's Holy Book called the Bible. This is so because the subject of prophecy in the book is directed at believers of the Christian faith, even though the subject may appeal to all observers of what is going on in our beloved country or the direction to which our country is heading. Also, Christianity is seen as the foundational religion of the nation even though other religions are equally accommodated in the country. Still, the majority of Americans see Christianity as their religion. Finally, we will be making references to the Christian Holy Bible because the Christian community is a political force to be reckoned with during elections and because the last presidential election tested the temperament of the Christian community.

Biblical Worldview

A worldview is a particular philosophical conception of the world. It is the fundamental cognitive orientation of an individual or society made up of the individual's or society's knowledge and point of view. It is a cultural phenomenon that comprises the individual's natural and acquired orientation. Thus, the Christian worldview includes the set of beliefs, attitudes, and behavioral patterns dictated by the Holy Bible. For the new Christian, the initial worldview conflicts with the biblical worldview, but this gradually changes as the new convert learns from the Bible and fellow Christians. At this stage, the natural patterns become submissive to the newly acquired set of beliefs that eventually change the individual's thinking, attitudes, and behaviors. With dedication and a supportive environment, the new Christian begins to grow in faith and exhibits new perspectives that give rise to new behaviors in conformity with the Christian faith. With these changes, the world starts to see him as a non-conformist.

Embracing the biblical worldview has a lot in common with an increase in the believer's faith. As the believer grows in faith, his attitude changes, which informs the behavioral change that is often witnessed in new converts. This transformation is due to an inner renewal that translates into outer change. This growth in faith leads to a gradual development of his worldview from the carnal to biblical; thus, the growth is not instant and not final, but a continuous process. The transformation may be smooth or turbulent depending on the pull exerted on the new convert from the opposing worldly community and the Christian community. There is always a degree of turbulence for every new convert unless the individual had a predetermined encounter with the Savior that brought about a sudden change in his perspective. The new convert will follow the worldview with the higher pull. If he has an enabling environment, he will continue to grow. But if the environment is not conducive for growth as a Christian, he will slide back into the carnal world that was his former domain. The new convert may develop into a full-grown Christian, or the growth may become stunted due to pressures and distractions from within the individual or from external forces. The challenges from the external forces can easily be overcome either by confronting the force with the truth or by fleeing from it. The challenge from within the individual is more formidable and very difficult to overcome until the individual submits to the Living Savior and allows the Holy Spirit to empower his spirit. All Christians are powerless without the indwelling of the Holy Spirit. When an individual has overcome the spirit within him (his flesh), he will be able to overcome the spirit that is outside of him (the devil). His ability to subdue the inner sinful urges will enable him to reject the outside pull. The individual that experienced half growth will develop a mixed worldview, and he is not on a solid footing because he will accept some Christian viewpoints and discard others. Eventually, he will go back to where he was in the beginning.

Some Christians' growth may be hampered by situations that may challenge their faith. When this happens, their growth may be halted, and they may stop growing. This stagnation in growth will also disturb the proper development of their worldview. The individual's inability to gain more knowledge for their development will result in losing the knowledge they previously gained, leading to developmental malnutrition and developmental atrophy. As the knowledge diminishes, the individual will be going about with a conjoined worldview that is dangerous for him and dangerous to Christianity. This type of individual will become confused and turn to apostasy.

Every Christian should watch out for individuals of this nature as they abound in our communities, and they abound in our congregations. We should try to discern the position of our Christian brother before we engage them in debates, not to talk of arguments.

It is not enough to be wary of actions that may cause controversy in the community of Christians. We must also watch out for the actors causing disaffection in the church because they need help. If they are not helped, they can pull down the whole congregation because they are ready tools in the devil's hands. However, these groups of individuals can be helped by mature Christians if their situation is well understood and re-routed to the right philosophy of Christianity. When well-refined, they will become good witnesses of the Christian faith. Every Christian should realize that trials and temptations abound. Also, bad things happen to godly people, and everything happens for a purpose that we may not understand until we see God. When trials come, we should wait patiently for God's intervention while relying on fellow Christians willing to offer support.

Christian Growth

We cannot discuss a biblical worldview without discussing the pattern of Christian growth that leads to a solid biblical worldview. The Bible admonishes Christians to grow in grace and the knowledge of our Lord Jesus Christ (2 Peter 3:18). Christian growth aims to make us be more like Christ daily. It is interesting to note that Christian growth is a continuous process, and it will not end or be complete until the Christian sees Christ

The Bible

face to face at the end of his life journey. Christian growth is attained through education and training, and these processes lead to transformation in both attitude and character, not the accumulation of diplomas or certificates. As explained earlier, Christianity is a way of life, and the Christian is expected to learn these ways and live them throughout his sojourn on earth. For education to be meaningful, there must be resources made up of teachers and other materials.

Teachers include those individuals who will inculcate the Christian life into the new Christian through teaching, preaching, and counseling under the authority and direction of the Holy Spirit. Other forms of teachers include those individuals who live the Christian life worthy of emulation by the growing Christian. This group includes pastors, preachers, sectional leaders, Christian families, and other growing Christians. The materials necessary for Christian growth include a Bible and daily dwelling in the Word (Bible) and other written Christian materials. His fellowship with other mature and growing Christians during study times, in prayer, and other church activities are also essential for the proper growth of a Christian. The growing Christian is also expected to enjoy periods of personal fellowship in worship, prayer, and study from the Bible. The experience with teachers is meant to guide him, while his personal experience while alone will deeply enrich his spiritual growth.

As the learner learns about the Christian life known as the walk, he also learns to "walk the walk" by practicing living the Christian life daily. However, learning cannot be possible without the enabling environment for learning and practicing what is being learned. Therefore, the learner is expected to move out of the carnal world into the Christian world, where he will be able to walk the walk without hindrance. Christian leaders are expected to be aware of the need for this type of environment to nurture Christian growth among new and growing Christians. After realizing this need, they should be able to prepare the available environment as an enabling environment for the growth process. The church environment should be conducive for learning and Christian growth, while the place of residence should be a Christian home. A Christian home should not necessarily be a mansion or a convent. Still, it should be an environment free of distractions or worldly attractions that can enable sinful acts or cause a growing Christian to backslide or return to his former state.

A newly converted Christian may not necessarily leave his physical place of abode, but there must be an emotional experience of the environment's transformation. Getting out of his usual place of abode (former world) does not indicate a lack of distraction, hindrance, or temptation. The appearance of these vices can be minimized and easily managed in a situation where the learner lives with other Christians, especially those who have passed through his present stage of growth and development. The environmental requirement described here is for a normal situation. A learner or new convert may be a husband or wife of an unconverted spouse. In this case, the learner must try to make the environment as conducive as possible while at the same time respecting the opinion of their spouse. The gentleness, respect, and understanding of the learner may be a useful factor in converting the partner. The learner may also benefit from godly advice and counseling from the elders of the congregation.

The Bible

An individual residing with elders who are yet to be converted must equally demonstrate respect while gently expressing their newly found faith to the elderly hosts. New converts should not condemn the faith of their old acquaintances but respectively reiterate the advantage or benefit being derived from their new faith. In both situations, new converts should not forsake the assembly of fellow converts where there is encouragement and opportunities to learn together from sharing of experiences. The most critical environmental challenge is the peer pressure that must be prayerfully resisted. New converts must shun being alone with unbelievers and only limit interactions to superficial levels. Those with bad social habits should resist the temptation of mingling with old friends who will encourage them to return to their sinful ways and at the same time discourage their newly found faith. New converts who have issues with addictions may contact mature Christians who have experience dealing with matters of this nature.

Many individuals grow up as nominal Christians. They are churchgoers, and they are morally upright without personal encounters with Jesus Christ. Also, some of them are not versed in the words of the Bible. This group of individuals needs to be helped with encouragement to build upon their past experiences. They need to be led to Christ, and they need the company of the Holy Spirit to accompany them in their Christian growth and bring illumination and clarity to their studies of the Bible. The familiarity with the workings of the Holy Spirit will give their lives a divine direction, and they will be able to discern good from evil. Christian teachers must realize that these groups of individuals have been in the carnal world for a long time despite bearing the title of a Christian. A gentle introduction to Christianity as a way of life different from this world's normal practices will help them appreciate where they are and the way they need to follow from the time they agree to follow Christ more closely. A good suggestion is to explain to them that they are on an adventure that takes them deeper into Christianity.

This slight digression into the Christian worldview is essential so that those individuals who call themselves Christians can look inward and identify their level of Christian growth. It is also critical for Christian leaders to judge if they are qualified to lead in a Christian community and if they are leaders, whether the counseling they are giving is objective or not. The Christian follower reading this may also be able to make an objective decision about who will lead them or who to follow. A Christian leader who can act as a counselor must have matured in knowledge and experience yet still be growing. In this case, the individual has identified his calling, knows his limitations, and will not hesitate to seek help or make referrals when necessary. It is the norm in every sphere of life for leaders to subscribe to continuous learning, give objective advice, and be humble enough to say so when they do not have the clue instead of providing wrong or misleading answers. They will not fail to seek help for themselves and others where they deem it necessary.

Implications of Christian Growth to Worldview

Just as growth determines performance in every sphere of life, developing a Christian worldview will depend on an individual's level of growth as a Christian. The common mistake people make is to equate church attendance with Christian growth. Church attendance and playing an active part in church activities are necessary for growth, but growth should be the driving force for church attendance and participation in church activities. Contrary to biblical directive, many servants of God have erred in hastily performing the laying-on of hands upon undeserving individuals (1 Tim. 5:22). For example, many individuals with talents have been mistakenly chosen to lead worship in many Christian circles when their Christian growth is nothing to write home about. We need talented men and women in the church, but more so, we need those whose talents have been translated into gifts. The Bible counseled that the mouth utters statements from the abundance in the speaker's mind (Luke 6:45). We can only give what we have, and the behavior experienced by every Christian is a reflection of the individual's growth as a Christian.

Every Christian is expected to be guided daily by the Christian culture of godliness with contentment, holiness in thoughts and actions, peaceful relationships with others, and love for family and neighbors. Strive and contention arise due to personal interests and the need to protect these interests. Christians should be conscious of adhering to biblical principles in all things and try as much as possible to accommodate others without compromising their faith. Every expression we make as Christians is a reflection of our Christian growth. It's either we are upright in our growth processes, or we have stopped growing. Our growth may be slow, or the growth can become stunted due to lack of proper nutrition from the Word or the feeder of the Word. We might have stopped learning; thus, our worldview is restricted to our knowledge of the Word, and in this case, we will continue to borrow from the carnal world to feed our opinions and arguments. If Christians fail to increase in knowledge from the Bible, their understanding will continue to diminish, and their worldview will become shallow. This development is perilous because that individual will begin to be tossed around by every wind of worldviews and guided by sentiments.

A well-grounded Christian, though still growing, will understand his position in Christ. He will recognize his opportunities and realize his limitations regarding issues involving a public debate. A mature individual will have a balanced worldview and not be involved in unnecessary discussion, debate, or arguments that often breed acrimony but do not solve any problem. Above all, he will avoid controversies that can cause disaffection between his brothers and sisters. He will abstain from every action that may turn his Father's house (Christian community) upside down. He will like to uphold the bond of peace that keeps the household of God together, and he will always cherish the Christian love that binds the brethren together. The mature Christian is expected to know the position of the church on worldly matters and be able to apply biblical principles in interpreting issues that arise in the world around him. Instead of becoming a contestant in matters of contention, he will prefer to be an agent of peace, rightly highlighting the merits and demerits of opposing views. Finally, he will create an impression of someone who can be turned to in matters that are confusing society.

Part II

Christianity And Prophecy

Christianity is a religion that came to being as an offshoot of Judaism. While Judaism is concerned with God's encounter with His elected people, the Israelites, and the promised coming of the Messiah, Christianity is concerned with the activities of the Messiah, the redemption of man as a consequence of man's sinfulness, and the phenomena of eternal life. Christianity consists of a set of beliefs known as doctrines. One of the doctrines of the Christian faith is the doctrine of prophecy. Prophecy is like a warning sign for every spiritually-minded individual. The unraveling of what will happen in the future is one of the adventures of a rationally-minded individual. Predicting what the future holds for a business motivates the businessman to make necessary plans to secure the future. In the same way, a spiritually-minded individual takes a spiritual excursion into the future and prepares for unforeseen circumstances.

There is a limitation to what the human mind can conceive. Because of the fear of what may happen when we refuse or fail to anticipate what the future has in store properly and because of the need to adequately prepare for eventualities, individuals have developed the habit of seeking spiritual means of looking into the future. It is reasonable to anticipate what is hidden in the future, which leads us to the art of predicting the future. When there is no vision, the people perish (Prov. 29:18A). Prophecy is a way of envisioning the future, and because of its supernatural nature, it is more potent than human imaginations if adequately harnessed. Prophecy has been with humanity for generations, and it serves as both a warning and a sign of comfort. It also prompts those who believe in it to take necessary actions.

Prophecy informs us about an oncoming event and warns about an impending danger, calamity, repercussion, or wrath that is a consequence of a punishable act or disobedience to supernatural authority. It serves as a sign or promise of good things to come, especially after a troublesome time. It also tells us about the plans of God for His world. Overall, it motivates the wise to take the necessary action. Prophecy also serves as the opportunity to experience God's presence and appreciate His Almightiness. Prophecy is the word or message delivered by the prophet to his human subjects following inspiration by a supernatural being or God. Most world religions engage in one form of divination or another as a way of looking into the future or hearing from the gods. In the instance of this book, prophecy is concerned with the practice in the Christian faith.

The issue of prophecy is complex, while the office of a prophet also requires a deeper form of inquiry. Most prophets are gifted, while only a few of them pass through the "school of the prophets." The school of the prophets is the experience gained by someone with the gift of prophecy in his quest to develop his giftedness. In this process, he learns the disciplines of the profession or calling, and he learns how to play the role of a prophet. The office of a prophet is sacred since the prophet is expected to act as the intermediary between his clients and God. In playing this role, he must be ready to conform to behaviors that are acceptable to God by acting as a servant of God. He must also minister to his client with utmost care under an environment of mutual trust and respect for one another. Finally, he must communicate his prophecies effectively while providing counseling service to his client to make his prediction impactful or valuable.

The Doctrine of Prophecy

Having delved into the growth and development of a Christian, we will now begin our discussion on one of the gifts that God has bestowed upon Christians and the church. Prophecy is about speaking forth what will happen in the future. It can also be defined as speaking forth what the Prophet wishes or expects to happen in the future. In this vein, prophets speak of comfort or good tidings that are expected to occur concerning individuals or a community. Prophecy can be confused with fortune-telling, depending on the person who delivers the prophecy or the source of the prophecy. Prophets prophesy while fortune tellers make predictions about a person's life. Fortune-telling has to do with the practice of divination, but the relationship between fortune-telling and prophecy is that the practitioners claim to represent higher authorities. Prophecy is usually attributed to a prophet who claims to be representing God. We are not going to be discussing the issue of fortune-telling because God forbids it.

A prophet of God acts as the mouthpiece or spokesperson for God. He does this by informing people about God's plan for His people on the one hand and speaking forth good tidings from his heart on the other hand. Speaking from a godly heart usually comes to pass, while speaking the mind of a prophet will depend on conditions like the faith and attitude of the recipient for the prophecy to become a reality. A godly heart is a heart that has been with God, and a person with a godly heart is a vessel for the conduit of God's grace. Prophecy may be for the present, but it is concerned about future events in most cases. Receiving from God and accurately delivering the message in the proper form, taking into cognizance the understanding and maturity of the receiver, requires some degree of knowledge and maturity on the part of the prophet.

The Prophet

A prophet is a person who prophesies or brings forth or speaks forth what will happen in the future. The prophet makes a spiritual excursion into the future different from someone who reads the present and makes projections about the future. The prophet is an intermediary between a god and humanity. In a religion like Christianity, the prophet speaks for God and speaks to God's children by declaring God's message. On the other way round, he talks to God about the needs of God's children. The message of the prophet is usually that of goodwill or a warning. The message can essentially be the promise of a reward or impending wrath. As a messenger of God, the prophet must deliver the message of God to the appropriate authority. He needs wisdom as he discharges this duty because many prophets have lost their lives while delivering God's messages in the past. Despite this hazard, the prophet must fear God far more than the receiver of the message, and he must neither add nor remove from the message.

In the days of the Bible, God's prophets delivered messages to kings. In most cases, kings paid visits to prophets when they were in distress. It was not common for prophets of God to be seen dining with the king or in the company of powerful men. Prophets of old would instead remain poor materially rather than lose their calling because of greed for material wealth. Their calling was sacred, and they kept their calling in high esteem just as they feared God Who had bestowed the gift on them. Spiritual gifts like the gift of prophecy and material gains are not compatible because the lust for material gain may rob the prophet of his sincerity of purpose. Unlike the prophets of old, present-day prophets canvass for attention in the public domain, and they display their relevance to the kings and people in high places. Many modern-day prophets have turned the calling of prophecy into a commercial activity; thus, the populace perceives the phenomenon of prophecy with mockery.

Prophets and Prophecy

A prophet is an individual who is supernaturally endowed with the gift of prophecy. All prophets prophesy or deliver prophecies. Any individual can be used for the delivery of prophecy. However, an individual delivering a prophecy is not necessarily a prophet. Prophecy is one of the five-fold ministries of the Holy Spirit (Eph. 4:11). It is also a spiritual gift (1 Cor. 14:1) bestowed on the church by the Holy Spirit for the church's edification. Those who are called into the ministry of prophecy are referred to as prophets, while the Holy Spirit can empower anyone to give prophecy. Apostle Paul encouraged Christians to desire the gift of prophecy because it is useful for exhortation, comfort, inspiration, correction, the revelation of secret sins, prediction of future events, and other revelations given to equip and for edifying the body of Christ (1 Cor. 14:3-4, 22, 24-25).

Prophecy reveals the mind of God to His people. It warns of an impending danger and actions that may be taken to avert the threat. Prophecy exposes sin and its consequences. It also announces God's goodwill toward His church. Overall, prophecy encourages Christians, strengthens faith in God, builds trust within the church, chastises sinners, comforts God's people, and rekindles hope for eternal life. The God of Christianity is a living God, and a living God is the One Who hears and speaks to His people. Prophecy is a confirmation that God has not forgotten His own, and it is a sign that God knows what His people are experiencing, whether pleasant or unpleasant. It is also a response to Christians' worship and prayers, showing that our God is responsive and He cares.

Prophecy And Other Doctrines

The Christian Bible contains many doctrines, and each of them is a classification of different themes of the Bible. An ardent Christian is expected to be aware of these doctrines, at least at the superficial level. In contrast, Bible teachers are expected to develop a more profound knowledge of these doctrines. The familiarity with these doctrines is necessary because the man of faith should be thoroughly versed in the understanding, meaning, significance, and application. Knowledge is essential because a teacher cannot give what he does not possess. Another important reason for studying Bible doctrines is that none of these doctrines work in isolation, but they work together and complement one another. For instance, the doctrine of prophecy helps our prayer life by providing illumination into our prayer requests.

Importance of Prophecy to Our Worship and Our Walk

Learning about prophecy will help Christians understand the attributes of God. The knowledge gained from the study of prophecy will help believers know how God acted in the past and relate it to their present circumstances. Understanding prophecy may also help us predict what God will do in a particular situation. If we are sure that our God is a deliverer, we can rest assured that He can deliver us from any trouble that may come our way. If we understand and believe that God makes everything work together for the good of His children, we will rest assured that He will intervene, and we will come out stronger from our unpleasant situation. When we realize that the God we serve will never share His glory with anyone, we will stop relying on men but rather keep our focus on God. This knowledge will enable us to recognize how awesome our God is and accord Him the worship He deserves. For this reason, the psalmist wrote in Psalm 107 verse 31 that men ought to praise the Lord always because of His goodness and His wonderful works.

Importance of Prophecy in Prayer

Prayer is about communicating with God. It is about appreciating God's promises and not merely requesting things that will satisfy our wants. It is about reminding God of His promises and appreciating Him for being mindful of us. The doctrine of prophecy clarifies our requests by re-routing us to the purpose of prayer. Prophecy also reveals to us our needs and helps us present our prayer requests in alignment with the will of God. Prophecy reminds us of God's promises, His acts in the past, and His ability to deliver us from our present predicament. Prophecy helps us not be selfish in our requests and not pray amiss. Just like worship, for which prayer is a part, prophecy helps us understand who God is, what He can do, and to what extent He can go on behalf of His children.

Importance of Prophecy to Our Knowledge of God

The Bible counseled that knowledge is the principal thing (Prov. 4:7). The knowledge of God transcends every other thing about the Christian life. Knowing what God can do and what He will not do inspires us to act with the fear of God as expected of us. This knowledge also allows us to leave at the hands of God the ideas that we do not understand and the problems that we have no power to solve. The understanding that God knows everything and can do everything is learned in the school of prophecy as we learn to wait upon Him and listen to Him during the quiet hour. The interaction between God and man as we speak to Him and listen as He speaks is the foundation for our everlasting relationship both now and in the hereafter.

Importance of Prophecy to Christian Leadership

Leadership in the Christian circle is different from leadership in the secular world because our Christian followers are the bride of the Lord and are therefore precious, while Christian leaders are their under-shepherds. Shepherds direct the sheep while under-shepherds receive instruction from the Great Shepherd about how to handle the flock of God. Since we cannot change individual believers, we rely on the Holy Spirit to bring about a transformation in their lives as we instruct them under God's divine direction. Prophecy helps us anticipate what is coming, gives ideas about what is to be done, and provides encouragement because we know that we are not alone. Through prophecy, we know the direction to lead the sheep, and we learn how to ask and receive on behalf of the sheep.

Sources of Prophecy

The subject of prophecy is spiritual, and prophecies are derived from the supernatural. Webster's Dictionary defined the supernatural as "something relating to an order of existence beyond the visible observable universe especially relating to God or a god, demigod, spirit, or devil." Since prophecy is from the supernatural, it is necessary to reiterate that it is from one of the sources mentioned above. From the perspective of Christianity, we believe that prophecy is either from God or the devil. Because anything that is not from God is from our adversary (the devil); there is no middle way, and a prophecy may come from either God or the devil. However, it is interesting to know that messengers of the devil can give accurate prophecies while godly men can also deliver prophecies from the devil. Because the devil is crafty, the so-called godly men can receive and deliver messages or prophecies given to them by the devil. Prophets who God appoints do deliver messages or prophecy from God.

Followers of the devil can receive authentic prophecies because Lucifer, also known as the devil, was formerly one of the heavenly angels before he was cast down to earth with his followers, according to the Bible (Isa. 14:12-14; Rev. 12:4, 7-9). Because of his past as a resident of heaven, he knows some secrets of the heavenly places. Moreover, because the devil is equally crafty and has experience in transmitting spiritual messages, he can send messages or transmit messages through unsuspecting, so-called messengers of God. This phenomenon is possible because these individuals are receptive to spiritual messages, and what they receive, they can transmit or reveal as prophecies. Therefore, every Christian who has the gift of receiving messages from God should be wary of this fact, and, of course, they should use discernment to interpret the messages that they receive in line with the Word of God. Apart from the gift of prophecy, the gift of discernment of spirit is invaluable for success in all the ministries of the Holy Spirit.

Every prophet of God must realize that things of the spirit can be corrupted, but the Word cannot be corrupted. The spirit can be faked, while the Word cannot be faked, except it is misinterpreted or misrepresented. When inconsistency occurs, an ardent student of the Bible will notice the difference. It is essential for messengers of God to seek and, if possible, to crave spiritual gifts, especially the gift of discernment of spirits. The gift of discernment of spirits will help them understand spiritual manifestations that are not from God. They will be able to differentiate between fake messages or prophecies and truthful ones. They will equally be able to separate Holy Spirit-filled messages, sermons, and teachings from those that are not, and men of God from messengers of Satan. For this reason, men of God ought to be always upright by refraining from worldliness, abstaining from sinful acts, being prayerful, and regularly meditating on the Word with absolute submission to the Holy Spirit.

Part III
A True Prophet

We initially defined the office of a prophet. Now we will examine the office of a true prophet. The only classical definition of a true prophet is the one declared in the Bible as someone who speaks, and his pronouncements become a reality. In the book of Deuteronomy chapter 18 verse 22, the mark of a true prophet was written as follows, "When a prophet speaks in the name of the Lord if the thing does not happen or come to pass, that is the thing which the Lord has not spoken; the Prophet has spoken it presumptuously; you shall not be afraid of him." Some true prophecies receive instant fulfillment, some get fulfilled with time, while some become a reality after the prophet's demise. Because of the timing of the fulfillment of prophecies, some prophets will be celebrated while still alive, while the work of others will receive appreciation long after their death. This definition from the Bible is one of the reasons why prophecy remains one of the controversial doctrines of the Christian faith.

The office of a prophet carries with it its own risk. The prophet may be mocked because of his prophecy, especially if his prophecies are against the people's wishes. He may also be assaulted or even killed for delivering God's message. The anticipation of death or assault would not deter a true prophet from carrying out God's assignment. Also, the love of material possession will not prevent a true prophet from proclaiming the truth of God's message. The true prophet is in partnership with God to whom he owes allegiance. He is spiritually rich though he may not be rich with material possessions. But he is spiritually rich because he is working for a rich God. He is an upright man, and he commands the respect of the populace. However, there is the danger of being carried away by the acceptance and respect of the people who may perceive him as a god because of the accuracy of his prophecies. Therefore, the prophet of God should be aware of this evil.

Analysis from the Definition

A prophecy from God always consists of two items, an action and a reaction. The promise of God's action is always contingent on man meeting certain conditions. Just like there is a reward for wrongdoing and another for doing what is right, God's prophecy is often attached to man's actions or inactions. For example, a warning to abstain from sin will result in a blessing for obedience (salvation) or eternal condemnation for disobedience. The first king in Israel was dethroned because of disobedience to the directive of the prophet of God (1 Sam. 13-15). The implication of this is that both God and man have roles to play in the fulfillment of prophecies. The good news is that God will always fulfill His part of the bargain. God is always faithful to His promises even when men are not.

A True Prophet

The crux of the matter in the fulfillment of prophecy is the sacred work of the prophet. A prophet must be willing to nurture the prophecy until fruition. A prophet who prophesies about rainfall must prepare for the rain, like in the story of Noah and the flood (Gen. chapter 6). Daniel (in Dan. chapter 9) was expectant of the fulfillment of Jeremiah's prophecy in Jeremiah chapter 25. Prophets of God have not completed their work until their prophecies are fulfilled. Prophets of God must be ready to watch over the brethren and nurture God's promises over their lives. Failure to do these places them in the same category as the fortune-tellers. A church leader who prophesies success and prosperity on children must equally provide an enabling environment for Christian upbringing that will enable them to use their God-given talents.

True Prophecy

As the term implies, a true prophecy denotes truthfulness in every circumstance surrounding the prophecy. It is a prophecy uttered by a true prophet as directed by God. A true prophet must have been with God and must have received the prophecy from God. The prophecy may appear wrong or not sensible in the prophet's thoughts, or it may also sound foolish to those receiving the prophecy, but the prophet must realize that the message is from God and must be delivered even when it does not make sense. After delivering the message, the prophet must return to God with thanksgiving for the opportunity to be used. The manifestation of the prophecy is not his problem, and he owes no mortal any apology for any fulfilled or unfulfilled prophecy. He also should not expect any praise for a fulfilled prophecy. Instead, he should ascribe all glory to God.

A true prophecy is a prophecy that comes to fulfillment. The fulfillment of prophecy also depends on the understanding of the receiver. The manifestation of God's promise must be anticipated, recognized, and accepted with a sense of appreciation. In most cases of what individuals describe as false prophecy or unfulfilled prophecies, the individual may not believe in the prophecy and then miss the manifestation. The receiver may not recognize the manifestation because he expects a different thing or have a different perspective. The fulfillment may be delayed, or it may be for another generation. Also, the fulfillment may not materialize because the individual did not fulfill his part of the bargain. We must never forget that God's promises are dependent on our obedience. When we trust Him and have faith in His ability to deliver on His promises, we will realize that He is a faithful God.

Prophetic Revelations

Prophets deliver the messages they receive or that are given or revealed to them. Like in the days of the Bible, the message received may be in the form of a written material handed over to the prophet or a call to write down some words or series of dictations (Ex. 31:18; Hab. 2:2-3; Rev. 1:19). God wrote the Ten Commandments on the stone tablets and handed them over to Moses for onward revelation to the people of Israel. In other instances, God spoke directly to individuals, like when God gave Moses instructions to confront Pharaoh in Egypt (Ex. 3:1-10). The Lord also instructed Moses to document or write down the wordings of a covenant that He made with the people of Israel (Ex. 34:27).

Especially in these modern times, prophets also receive their messages through visions and dreams. Visions are vivid images that are short, sharp, and convincing to the individual perceiving them. These messages are received when the prophet is awake and fully conscious (Isa. 1:1; Hab. 1:1). In some instances, the prophet also actively participates in the event (Rev. 1:10-20). Prophets also receive revelations through dreams during their sleep (Dan. 7:1). The message may either be short or long. However, the subject of dreams is controversial because it needs interpretation, and the interpretation of dreams is a gift on its own. Therefore, the prophet must be careful in his revelation of the prophecy received during his sleep in that he must be sure of its meaning. Finally, it is reasonable to describe the vision as a dream if he is unsure of its meaning. Both the dreamer and the receiver of a message received in a dream need the help of God to decipher the true meaning of the dream.

Prophetic Utterances

Prophecies are usually delivered in two forms. The first method is when prophets deliver their messages in spoken words when physically in the flesh. That means they received the messages and had time to pray over the message, interpret it, and prepare their mode of delivery. A good example is the one involving Prophet Nathan and King David (2 Sam. 12:1-12). Here the prophet used a parable to hone home his message. Situations like this make it possible to prepare for the conversation because many prophets were persecuted, and some lost their lives during their assignments (2 Chron. 24:17-21; Jer. 26:20-23). John the Baptist was equally murdered because he confronted the truth in the case involving King Herod Antipas and his queen, Herodias (Mark 6:14-29). Some prophecies or the whole meaning of some prophecies may not be understood by the prophet or the person receiving the message. Therefore, the ability of the prophet to interpret the prophecy may require divine intervention.

The second delivery method for prophetic messages is also verbal, but in this case, the messenger speaks under the influence of a spirit as in a trance. For example, the individual can make utterances during a church service, like during worship sessions or prayer time. In this case, the statement can be directed at a particular individual, group of people, or situation. The message can also be general, and the individual concerned is expected to understand the message. The tricky part of this type of message delivery is that the "prophet" may not remember what transpired during his trance, or he may not understand his prophetic utterances. Another problem with this type of message is that many individuals may key into it, whereas the message may not be directed at them. Prophets who are materialistic exploit this form of prophetic messages to prey on their followers. In a congregation with numerous gifts, elders are usually available to help individuals concerned with the literary meaning of prophecies.

Fulfilled Prophecies

One factor that makes the Bible and the religion of Christianity unique is the subject of prophecy. The history of the Israelites is a good starting point for the study of biblical prophecy. There are many fulfilled prophecies in the Bible, but the greatest of all is the one concerning the people of Israel and their role in the salvation of humanity. The life of our Lord, Jesus Christ, His birth, ministry, death, and resurrection are classic examples of fulfilled prophecies. These fulfilled prophecies form the basis for the Christian faith, and they are the reasons for the belief in the expected return of the Messiah that was equally predicted. In turn, these fulfilled prophecies form the basis for the belief in the promise of eternal life that is the hope for all adherents of the Christian faith.

Understanding fulfilled prophecies is dependent on the familiarity with the God Who made the promise and having trust and faith in His ability to deliver on His promises. Faith in God's promise is helped by knowing His past actions because He can repeat what He has done in the past and has the power to do what He has promised to do. A good understanding of the will of God will help us understand His plans for us and His ways of doing things. For example, when we find ourselves in troubled situations, we know that He is able, and He will surely deliver us. Also, when we are deep in sin, and He promised judgment for unrepentance, we must quit sinning because we know that God punishes sinners. The best way to appreciate God's ability to fulfill what He promised is to allow Him to play His act as He wishes instead of confining His interventions into a set of popular actions.

Unfulfilled Prophecies

The issue of unfulfilled prophecy introduces another area of controversy into the subject of prophecy. While the case of prophecy involves the pronouncement by the prophet, fulfilled prophecy is determined by the occurrence of what was predicted. From our analysis of the definition of prophecy, we can deduce that the outcome of a prophecy depends on other factors that are not within the prophet's control. For example, the prophet cannot play God's role, and he cannot replace the individual concerned with the prophecy. It is essential to realize that only the power behind the prophecy can bring about the fulfillment of the prophecy. Another vital factor to consider is that the work of prophecy places a burden on the prophet in that as a prophet, he owes it a duty to nurture the prophecy into maturity. Having visualized the vision, he must keep watch until a physical manifestation. Doing this involves informing the people, praying, meditating, and encouraging the people to remain faithful as they await the promise of God. For example, Noah continued to pray, preach, and work until the manifestation of the prophesied flood (Gen. 6).

In describing what can be considered an unfulfilled prophecy, we must examine the significant factors concerned with the prophecy. We must consider the work of the prophet, the words of the prophecy, and the people receiving the prophecy. The prophet must be a man of integrity expected of a prophet, the prophecy must be delivered as it was given, and the people receiving the prophecy must be receptive, obedient, patiently await the fulfillment, and be able to recognize the fulfillment when it occurs. The first phenomenon that people consider an unfulfilled prophecy is when the fulfillment is not as expected. For example, in the fulfillment of the prophecy concerning the birth of Jesus Christ, the Jews were expecting a physical liberator. Still, God sent a spiritual liberator because spiritual liberation must precede physical liberation for the total emancipation of all humanity.

Another form of unfulfilled prophecy to consider is when the prophet prophesied "ex cathedral" by playing God. For example, some prophets give a time limitation for the manifestation of their prophecies, forgetting that only God has time and seasons under His control. Prophets of God should learn from the wisdom of Apostle Paul that we know in part, and we should prophesy in part (1 Cor. 13:9). The final point to consider in unfulfilled prophecy is when the prophet is a false prophet. These prophets arrogate spiritual power to themselves, and they claim to be prophets and miracle workers. Though some of their prophecies come to fulfillment, most of their pronouncements are meant to confuse the public. The confusion that they cause results in frustration and disappointment for those who trust in them. For those in this category who claim to be Christians, the havoc that they inflict makes adherents of their faith movements lose their faith, while their escapades become a tool for the critics of the Christian religion.

Timing and Prophecy

As stated earlier, the outcome of a prophecy may be immediate or delayed until a future date. It may materialize after the prophet's demise, while the prediction may also be for the coming generation. For instance, the prophecy concerning the flood came to fulfillment when the prophet and those who received the prophecy were still alive. The prediction concerning the coming of Jesus Christ became fulfilled when the prophets and the receivers were all dead and gone. The prophecy that comes to pass when the prophet is still alive brings credibility to the prophet's work, while the one that does not become fulfilled immediately does not discredit the prophet. Still, it will keep him humble as he continues to serve his Master. He may also become demoralized unless he keeps his eyes on the Person Who called and sent him. As stated earlier, the pitfall for the prophet whose prophecy becomes fulfilled is the tendency to be puffed up or turned into a god by his followers.

The followers of the prophet equally have expected behaviors to prophecies that become manifested immediately or later. For the predictions that enjoy immediate manifestation, the followers will rekindle their faith and become more committed to God and the prophet. This commitment deserves a humane understanding because the followers are prone to abuse. At the same time, the prophet may also play on their submissiveness, turning them to "robots" and start making bread out of the brethren. The prophecies that have a delayed manifestation are meant to teach believers the habits of waiting upon the Lord and longsuffering. Too much waiting can also sway believers from their position of faith, thereby becoming faithless (Prov. 13:12A). Weariness can make believers lose their faith in both God and His prophets. This condition deserves pragmatic management by the prophet or the shepherd in charge of the community. The general attitude of believers to delayed or unfulfilled prophecies will be to keep their hope upon the Lord, especially if they were well-grounded in faith through the knowledge of the words of God.

God's Intervention in the Affairs of Men

It is essential to know that God's sovereign purpose and will rule in the affairs of men. This rulership works according to His divine plans. Even though God is a patient listener to men's conversations, He does not get involved in debates or arguments between individuals and groups of people. Instead, He makes every situation work to achieve His purpose, just as He makes situations both pleasant and unpleasant to work for the ultimate good of His children. Also, God raises and brings down nations and individuals to fulfill His purposes. His purposes and plans can become visible to us if we can take a broader look at events instead of looking at individuals or participants. Making a retrospect journey into the history of humanity, "godly men" have led God's people to their defeat and destruction. At the same time, God has also used "ungodly men" to bless and deliver His people. In a situation that we as humans do not have any control over, the reasonable thing to do is to look unto God for supernatural intervention and submit to His will instead of looking unto men and being disappointed.

Every day around us, we encounter individuals praying for interventions and blessings from God. Like any good judge, God listens to every case and apportions solutions to individual and corporate wishes according to His predetermined plans. This one sounds curious, but just like any judge will deliver judgment according to the Constitution, God also answers prayers and apportions rewards according to His will. Some of

His will can be found in the written Word, the Bible, as well as by the inspiration of His Holy Spirit. Another point to consider is the issue of mercy. Earthly rulers can decide to use promulgation of mercy on a condemned offender. The Lord, our God, can also choose to be merciful to anyone as He pleases (Rom. 9:15). These actions are also part of His predetermined plans. In two areas in the Bible, God decided to dialogue with humans. In the first instance, God engaged in a conversation concerning His judgment pronounced on the city of Sodom and Gomorrah (Gen. 18:16-33). God had already made up His mind because of all He had heard and seen. Remember that our God has the attribute of omniscience. Another area of dialogue was during the reign of King Hezekiah (2 Kings 20). Even though God prolonged the king's days, the days were days of preparation for an oncoming national calamity. The added fifteen years were days of preparation for his death, and just as the Bible says, a day to the Lord is like a thousand years. Thus, the decision of God did not change anything for the king.

The Call to Be a Prophet

Every service to God is a calling, and every believer is called to the service of the Lord through service to fellow human beings. Those who appreciate the calling see it as a privilege, and they strive to justify their callings. Firstly, it is essential to know that prophets are called by God, not by individuals (Jer. 1:5). They are called for a purpose (John 15:16), and those called are expected to live holy lives (1 Peter 1:15-16). Prophets of God are expected to be humble in the conduct of their ministerial appointments and their practices, devoid of arrogance or greed. They are equally not expected to boast of any power or accomplishment because they represent God as the conduit of His grace (1 Cor. 4:7). Instead of greed and arrogance, they are expected to return the glory of their accomplishments to God Who chose, empowered, and assigned them. Prophets and other workers who enjoy the callings of God are expected to justify their callings by recognizing that they are being called by the name of the Lord. Thus, they are representatives of God. They are expected to live holy lives and depart from iniquities (2 Tim. 2:19). They must realize that God is the source of their power and that the success in their ministry depends on God. Therefore, they should not be involved in unnecessary arguments, especially political arguments that may divide the church of God or pit individuals or groups against one another (2 Tim. 2:23; Titus 3:9). They should rely and depend on God for all things and give glory to God for everything He accomplished through them (Isa. 42:8). The grace attached to the title is their sufficiency.

Many prophets were not called to the ministry by God. Some are called by other prophets or pastors because they have the spiritual gift of prophecy or because they occasionally manifest the gift. The Bible warned that church elders should not be hasty to lay hands on individuals or in the appointment of ministers (1 Tim. 5:22). Hastily laying on of hands or appointing a minister without confirmation of the calling is a sinful act that will attract repercussions. Some call themselves simply because they think they can play the role or believe they have the gift. Some in this group may have the gift, but they lack the training that will help them develop the gift and learn the tools of the calling. In Christianity, all prophets who God does not call are merely trading with the gift of God.

The Modern-Day Prophets

As stated earlier, the gift of prophecy is a blessing to humanity, while godly prophets are a gift to the church. Knowledge brings about prosperity, and prosperity in the world depends on knowing what is to come and preparing for it. Prophets can foresee what is to come, and the wise will make adequate provision to either hide in the day of calamity or reap in the day of prosperity. Since prophecy is an excellent gift to be desired and prophecy is promising, popular, and brings about prosperity (not necessarily financial prosperity), many people like to become prophets. The zeal to become a prophet or develop the ability to prophesy has brought about many prophets in our time. Some possess the gift and are making godly use of their skills. Many others possess the gift, but they have never passed through the "school of prophets." They never learned under the tutelage of a mentor nor learned under the discipline of the Holy Spirit; thus, they are undisciplined in their actions.

Others are neither called to be prophets nor possess the gift of prophecy, but they are professionals who intend to reap the benefits of being a prophet through hook and crook. This last group of prophets deceives the public through propaganda or resorts to magic for their miracles and hypnosis. Individuals in the first group who are godly and disciplined do not get involved in controversies. Those in the second group who are untutored are not disciplined and regard their calling as a profession. They advertise their trade and crave popularity to enjoy good patronage. They are popular because of their advertisements and their promise of material prosperity to the unsuspecting public. They promise material prosperity for those who can contribute materially to their business. The final group mimics the activities of the second group that though possesses the gift lacks the training and discipline of the called. They also advertise their trade, but the fact remains that they are not original because they never possessed the gift, and they are not called to be prophets.

The bottom line is that a true and godly prophet needs no advertisement. They are reserved, and they have a reverent fear for the Giver of every good gift (1 Cor. 4:7). They know that they are working in the vineyard of the Master and realize that a day is coming when they will have to give stewardship of their activities. In essence, they always remember to glorify God in all that they do. Others are not like that; they lack this knowledge; thus, they arrogate all power to themselves and receive a reward for their work by robbing the people – making bread out of brethren. Those who have the gifts and rob society have already got their rewards, and they have nothing waiting for them in eternal life. The fake prophets will also receive their just reward.

Part IV

The Human Experience

Experience over the years has shown that Christianity is evolving or Christians are reshaping Christianity by responding to the tide of time. Also, as the world around us is changing, so are Christians and Christianity. For instance, technological advancement makes it possible to broadcast Christian services to many listeners and observers over a large expanse of areas, at times covering continents. The modes of worship, especially the conduct of church activities, are changing, and the roles of church workers are equally evolving to meet the needs of the modern church. The sermon styles are equally changing, and society's needs often dictate the sermon topics. Thus nowadays, the central subject of many sermons has to do with blessings and breakthroughs. It appears that the significant purposes of scriptures have been forgotten while the myopic preachers see financial blessings as the major need of society today.

The Bible warned of the appearance of these days, the days when fake preachers will abound, and preachers will deviate from teaching the "Truth" or the true words of God and instead preach what society dictates. These days, listeners have developed itchy ears and are happy to receive the words that are not meant to save their souls but rather the words that will satisfy their carnal desires. Among this category of preachers are formally faithful preachers of the Word who decided to join the modern-day preachers because of the financial inducements. Others joined the group because they had not been properly groomed in the art of ministry. Thus, they follow the new trend in town. Most modern-day preachers were not called into the ministry, but they are in it to make a living.

The message of the Bible is clear to every ardent and curious investigator. But many present-day messengers of the gospel have changed the outlook of the clergy from what it previously was. The preachers of old were more concerned about the condition of the minds of men and the sanctity of their souls, while modern-day preachers are more concerned about the comfort and well-being of their followers that will flow back to them. While the preachers of old were singing "the old rugged cross," the modern-day preachers are singing "Abraham's blessings are mine." The words of the Bible remain unchanged, but the attitude of believers has changed tremendously over the years. It is difficult to say whether the brethren changed the clergy or the brethren were changed by the quality of the clergy. But one clear thing is that Christians have been advised not to conform to this world or be occupied by the affairs of this world (Rom. 12:2), but to look forward to a future life preserved for them in the world to come.

The Human Experience

Experience from a Global Perspective

Preying on people under the guise of religion is not confined to any region. Apart from the basic human needs of food, shelter, and clothing, human necessities can also be classified under local, regional, and universal needs. While food, shelter, and clothing are universal needs, peaceful existence and the absence of wars and other calamities form the needs specific to some regions. For example, I am privileged to have lived in Nigeria in West Africa, where the majority of the inhabitants are religious. By the way, being religious does not translate into holiness. The Bible will determine the definition of holiness on the one hand and the person defining on the other hand. The country's inhabitants rely on prophecies for many reasons, just as they pray to God for everything, including mundane things like restoring power supply by the power generating authorities after a power outage. Individuals also pray for the payment of salary arrears owed by their employers, including the government. The people have been emasculated to the extent that they rely on God for almost everything. The Bible employed every believer to rely on God in everything, but this reliance does not prevent us from the judicious use of the resources He has entrusted into our hands.

People have become perplexed because of the poor management of the political and economic environment as they now find solace in religion. People have become desperate, and prophets are having a field day milking the society of the little left with them. Individuals who are living in developing nations like Nigeria pray to God for food supplies because they do not know when the next meal will arrive. They also pray for healing from diseases because healthcare facilities are not functioning, and only the privileged can afford the few available and functional private hospitals. They equally pray for protection from robbers and bandits because the law enforcement agencies have failed miserably to discharge their responsibilities. Instead, they rely on prophets and divinators to solve these recurrent problems, and these divinators claim to have answers to these myriads of problems. Unfortunately, when their prediction fails, they blame the poor believer that he is not holy enough to receive from God. This practice has been their usual excuse because no man can blame God. Blaming God is referred to as blasphemy that is punishable even by death in some religious circles.

Yet another example. I have been living in the Western world for about two decades. During this period, I've monitored the religious activities of the inhabitants of the nations. For example, many residents of the USA are equally religious but not as religious as Nigerians. Americans have a scientific orientation, and in America, being a civilized society, common problems like food supply, healthcare, and security are being taken care of by the government. Though Americans also pray, they do not pray due to the scarcity of meals. Also, they approach healthcare institutions for available and affordable healthcare because of the effectiveness of government policies. However, this does not mean that they do not pray for healings. Americans also have found ways of looking into the future through prophecies and divinations. They believe in seeking what the future holds, but not in terms of mundane things for which individuals in poorly managed nations pray. Average American prayer points are prosperity, love, and relationships in most cases. The majority do not seek spiritual help for daily needs like the Nigerians do.

It also appears that individuals in poorly managed economies seek God more. Poverty is a powerful tool in the hands of Satan, and impoverished people have nobody to look unto for their predicaments except God. The spiritual experience of inhabitants of these nations in our example is similar. However, their priorities are different when we look at the roles of prophets and their prophecies in their political systems. Politicians in both countries depend on support from spiritual organizations. And they have been benefitting from their votes and goodwill in terms of prayers and prophecies. During elections, politicians also enjoy the support and votes from members of these spiritual organizations. Religious groups derive some benefits from politicians as they fulfill the promises made before elections. But the objective facts remain that politicians will not act beyond their philosophical beliefs of satisfying the largest majority of the populace. Thus, the demands of the religious groups may be partially met or not met at all.

When Prophecy Goes Awry

A true prophecy does have a meaning, and it will come to pass or become fulfilled no matter how long it may take. The interpretation of prophecy is entirely a different dimension in biblical prophecy. Prophecy interpretation is of particular significance when the prophet delivers the message crudely. However, a prophecy that is well-explained needs no interpretation. The receiver of prophecy must be a believer in the prophet or who and what the prophet represents. He must be a student of the Word and understand the subject of prophecy. Thus, he must be able to test the prophecy. The receiver of prophecy may request clarification from the prophet or humbly proceed to the mercy seat of God for a divine revelation. The latter part is recommended for every clever child of God because only God is omniscient and unchangeable while human beings have limited knowledge, and we are prone to change.

Prophetic messages may be pleasant or unpleasant, or they may be good news that brings happiness and joy or bad news that makes the receiver afraid and seek redress in the court of the Lord. While the prophet is obligated to deliver the message, the receiver must be prepared to receive the message with humility. The time may be long enough for individuals to miss the manifestation of a prophecy or confuse the interpretation or both. An extended period of waiting may equally divert the attention of a believer, but the promise of God is not only to bring relief but also to train the individual. Maturity in faith, trust, and belief in God, endurance, and perseverance at the personal level toward becoming a well-rooted believer always accompany these experiences.

Prophets are human beings, and they are fallible men. Men do change, and it is only God Who does not change. The revelation of a prophet and the delivery of his utterances are subject to the person's physical, mental, and spiritual state. A prophet should know the importance of being an upright person in the presence of God else he will be seen as an ex-anointed prophet. A prophet in this category may still possess the gift of prophecy, but his prediction may not be as accurate as it used to be. A prophet must be of sound health so that his failing health may not blur his perceptions. He must also learn to live above temptation because temptation may obscure his sense of rational reasoning that he may become corrupted. Any individual who falls into the net of a prophet who is not in right standing with God may receive a message that is tainted with error. It should be noted that error in prophecy is not from God. It is within the domain of the prophet.

A Prophetic Case Study

The story of King Ahab and the lying spirit is a good case in the study of prophecy. Though the story appears controversial, this is not unusual because this is not the only time recorded in the Bible that a spirit approached God for permission to do what can be considered evil. The first example involves Satan's permission to try Job, a man described as blameless and upright (Job 1:1-12). God permitted Satan to try Job, but Job passed the test, and at the end of the story, we saw a triumphant Job giving glory to God. Our God can see the end from the beginning. He permitted Job to be tested and supplied the strength for Job's endurance, and He was not disappointed in His servant. Every mature Christian believes that God controls everything that happens in a man's life, whether pleasant or unpleasant (Deut. 32:39).

The case of King Ahab followed a similar direction to the story of Job in that a spirit requested permission to work on the king's prophets. God knew King Ahab and the expected outcome of his reign. Even though King Ahab had a prophet of God in his domain, he did not like the prophet's counsel because it was against his opinions. God's will is not expected to fall in line with the views of men because God is not a respecter of persons, and He is also not a friend of habitual and compulsive sinners. The prophet of God remained truthful to his calling by informing the king of God's plan even though the king despised his sayings. But the king preferred the revelations from the bootlicking prophets surrounding him, and because he did not like the truth, God allowed his prophets to give him a lie camouflaged as the truth. He did not listen to the true prophet in his stubbornness but instead sent him to jail.

The end of King Ahab has become history and a lesson for every student of the Scripture. He listened to his prophets and met with his doom. The question that comes to mind is whether they lie in heaven or not. The answer is straightforward. Heaven is not a place for emotions, and in heaven, everything is naked before God, so there is no need for lying. Issues like lying or withholding the truth are confined to this sinful world. It is also pertinent to know that human affairs are subject to heavenly control. It is important to note that prophets are messengers concerned with relaying messages from the above stories about heavenly transactions. The idea of acting as message modulators or playing the roles of debate moderators does not appear to be part of their assignments.

This realization of heavenly transactions shows that prophecy is not the end of everything, and God is the ultimate in everything. Those individuals who build their lives upon prophecy should be wary of these stories. Individual cases are between them and their Creator or God. The prophet of God has no solution to anyone's problem unless to perform activities that God directs. A prophet who portends to possess answer to people's problems is claiming to be a god and should be feared because he has a supernatural power that is not from the God of all creation. That kind of prophet may be an agent of Satan. He is likely one of the false prophets described in the early part of this book. A good piece of advice for every student of prophecy is to be upright with God, receive prophecies humbly if there are any, and always seek the face of God for divine revelation.

When Only the Best Matters

The stories above demonstrated two contrasted incidences. First, the story of Job was an example of man's submission to God's sovereign will. God's action for permitting the trial of Job by the devil and God's testing was received philosophically by Job as his deserved fate. Despite all that he went through, he did not feel any anger against God, and despite pleas to forsake God, he stood his ground on his faith in God and in his belief that every servant of God must be ready to receive whatever God sends their way (Job 2:10). This example should be in the mind of every believer of God. Unfortunately, few Christians are willing to live the experience of Job and still believe in God. Most Christians nowadays follow God because of what they want to receive from Him and not their love for the Lord.

Secondly, the story of King Ahab is an example of man's desire for prophecies that only suit his purpose. It is like a man who made his plan without consultation with God and then sought God's approval. It can also be likened to a young boy who destroyed his toy and then asked his father to repair it, directing him how to do it. The king was not interested in what the Lord proclaimed through His prophet. Instead, he preferred the prophets who would declare his personal choices. This example is what is being repeatedly played in Christian circles today. The unfortunate thing is that many prophets are ready to dance to the tunes of their followers. So many prophets of today are men's pleasers and not pleasers of God.

Prophet's Incursion into Politics

Like every other individual, politicians like to have an insight into the future, and one way of doing this is through the work of prophets. They want to hear prophets' opinions and God's plan during elections. Receiving an endorsement from a famous prophet with support from Christians or church groups is bound to boost the electability of any politician. Thus, the involvement of prophets in the campaign strategies of a politician serves two purposes. On the one hand, it assures the politician of eligible voters, and on the other hand, it gives him a form of spiritual approval from the clergy. Christian organizations participate in politics or offer support to politicians or political groups because they need to preserve the church and its role in the nation. Importantly, Christians owe it a duty to promote Christian virtues, and the best way to do this is to offer support to a politician who will promote these ideals. However, Christian groups support candidates with their votes and pray for their success at the polls. The area of prayer is where the idea of prophecy comes in.

The majority of countries that are founded on Christian values always see the preservation of Christian values as a huge topic of discussion during electioneering campaigns. The people want to hear about the religious life of the candidates and how they intend to treat the church and respect and preserve Christian values. Some countries also have Christian

The Human Experience

political groups and parties whose members contest elections. Examples of values represented include the role of the family, euthanasia, abortion, and the separation of the church and the state. Every electable candidate must be ready to present sensible answers to questions on these topics if they intend to curry the favor of Christian groups. The incursion of Christians into the political arena brings about the involvement of prophets in politics. The necessity of Christians who can vote is a significant gain for politicians, but the addition of Christians who can pray and prophesy increases politicians' faith in their ability to become successful during elections.

Prophets and National Politics

God has been known to appoint kings over His people from ancient times. The Gentile nations also had a way of installing and removing kings. The Bible's examples show the role of prophets in the life and times of biblical kings. We find examples of kings who benefitted from God's assistance and direction, and we see those who abandoned the God of the Bible and the repercussions of their actions. Gentile nations also had gods who helped them in all their activities, including wars, and we read about the failures of these gods whenever they contended with the living God. It is in God's character to appoint prophets for His people and nation, and He delivered His messages to the nations through these prophets. The present-day leader of nations also enjoys this benevolence from God, especially those who rely on the sovereignty of God.

Most nations of the world are blessed with godly prophets who reveal God's mind to individuals in the position of power.

Many of these prophets reveal their predictions for the year as it concerns nations and the entire world. Most world leaders have spiritual advisers who link them to prophets who can be trusted, but most politicians may not adhere to the prophecies from these prophets. Their choices are made out of the need to take politically correct actions against the people they govern. Also, they prefer to take steps that will supply the common good of the populace, even when those actions contradict the will of God. Most leaders do not fail because of the lack of spiritual and intellectual counselors. They fail because they would not listen to instructions. God's ways and thoughts are different from ours, just like He used those things that we count as foolishness to confound individuals that are judged to be wise (1 Cor. 1:27). God's messages are for spiritual individuals because the messages are designed to be spiritually discerned (1 Cor. 2:14).

The Church and Politics

The church is a socio-cultural group, and as inhabitants of a polity, they are expected to partake in politics both as voters and contestants. The general belief that Christians should not participate in politics is a misnomer. The church is not expected to be partisan, but individual members can play active roles in politics. Also, the church is not expected to impose political candidates on members or form any political alliance with any political party. Forming a political union with a political group will make the church become an affiliate that can be praised for the success of a regime or blamed for the failures of the administration. The church's involvement in an alliance with a political group is a deviation from the church's roles of presenting individual members ready for the second coming of Jesus Christ. During the voting exercises, Christians are simply exercising their civic rights, while as contestants, they will be representatives of their group and the larger society. In a country where there is a constitutional separation of church and state, the church has little effect on politicians apart from the standard transactions ensuing between the voter and the voted. Still, as a participant, the Christian politician may influence the government's policy for good.

Since the church is a spiritual organization and politics is the way of the world, the church needs to exercise caution when dealing with politicians. The church should make it a rule that it is not a partisan organization and should not allow politicians to infiltrate the church. Church members should not be divided for anything temporal. Allowing church members to become polarized is allowing division into the body of Christ that will enable the devil to enter into the midst of believers. Because of the need to preserve the bond of the Spirit that unites the church, the relationship between the church and politicians should be platonic. Political debates should never be allowed in the church, but church members are free to have political affiliations. Honest and God-fearing men and women from the church may present themselves for political offices and thereby influence society for good to the extent that the name of God can be glorified. But, allowing politicians to have their way in the church will result in disaffection among members while the church will be turned into a political tool in the hands of politicians.

Part V

The Assault on the Church

As described earlier, prophecy, like other gifts, is a blessing to the church and the nation. But prophecy, if not correctly used or its practice not jealously guarded, may lead to peril. The prophet may be harmed while the populace may be exploited. To put it succinctly, what happened during the 2020 presidential election in America was an assault on the church of God. Here we witnessed the abuse of the doctrine of prophecy whereby many Christians believed in the prophecy that one of the candidates had been chosen to win the election. Unfortunately, many others on the opposing side did not believe in this prophecy widely circulated by word of mouth and through the news media. Moreover, the prophecy surrounding the election generated interest among Christians worldwide, and interestingly, believers from other parts of the world were also divided because of this prophecy. It is a fact that many nations of the world depend on the outcome of the presidential election in the USA as a form of barometer for the formulation of its foreign and domestic policies. This reality explains the involvement of foreigners in the controversy.

The result of the imbroglio was a great division in the body of Christ. Families were turned against each other while church members argued and hated each other. All this happened because politicians infiltrated the church, Christians lost their guard, the under-shepherds lost control, and the sheep were allowed to stray away. The primary topic of discussion in the church arena is no longer salvation, Christian living, and eternal life, but politicians and politics. The Christian fathers who understood what was going on were perplexed. It looks as if they folded their arms with their mouths shut while they opened their eyes and watched the assault on the church of God. But they were praying for Christians and the church because some of them had once prophesied about the assault. This type of incident can only happen when the practice of prophecy is not regulated, which has led to the proliferation of the practice to the detriment of the unsuspecting public.

How Did We Get Here?

One adage says it is easier to get into a bad habit but challenging to get out of it. As described earlier, prophecy is a blessing to the church. However, building our lives on prophecy alone is a bad practice. We have realized that all the doctrines of Christendom are essential for the Christian life, and relying on only one of them is dangerous. The Bible represents the Christian map for the Christian journey. But looking to a page for success in the journey of a lifetime is both foolish and dangerous. The love of God precedes the love for the Bible, while the knowledge that God is all in all precedes the understanding of the Bible. We can know the Bible and fail at its interpretation concerning a particular problem or situation. But the knowledge of God will help us understand that the Spirit can help us understand all things. Still, the Holy Spirit is available to help us with the wisdom to understand and apply biblical principles to our daily lives. Also, the knowledge of the entire Bible precedes the knowledge about biblical prophecy because we cannot treat one in isolation from the other.

We cannot portend to be a master of prophecy without having the knowledge of the Bible and relying on the power of the Holy Spirit. We need to understand the mind of God that is revealed in His will before we can successfully interpret any prophecy with utter reference to the words of God contained in the Bible. Believing in ourselves is throwing caution into the wind, and we must realize that the devil abounds anywhere the Holy Spirit is not present (1 Sam. 16:14-15). A prophet may easily miss the mark of accurate prophecy when he loses his guard. A group of prophets may miss the mark when they are emotionally involved in the outcome of the prophecy. A prophet may equally fail in the art of making accurate prophecy when he joins others or relies on the counsel of other prophets without due recourse to the sovereignty of the Spirit of God. Also, a whole generation of prophets may equally miss the mark when they turn their sacred calling into a political tool. A prophetic message is between God and His prophet and not with a group of prophets, even though different prophets may come up with the same predictions. This phenomenon only shows that God is not an author of confusion.

Putting Things in the Right Perspective

The Bible counseled Christians to get knowledge and understanding (Prov. 4:7). The first step in understanding what and why things went wrong is to analyze what happened in comparison with an acceptable standard. When something unusual happens, the usual reaction is to be attracted to one's opinions and choices, which is the way of every rational mind. In this way, individuals may be wrong in their thinking or actions, but they have acted on their understanding of the situation. Doing otherwise is an aberration to the normal. The other way of reasoning is to rely on superior knowledge to illuminate the circumstance before making a rational decision. Following this way can be achieved by approaching someone who has a better understanding of the situation, like a counselor, or seeking the intervention of someone who can foresee the future like a fortune teller or a divinator. The two classes mentioned above are carnal ways of behavior as opposed to the conduct of a spiritual-minded individual.

The spiritually-minded individual will commit every situation to the hand of God. Though curious or troubled, he will seek the face of God and will be ready to accept the verdict as the will of God, believing that everything will work out according to the plan of God for his ultimate good. In areas of deep need or a more profound understanding of the will of God, he may seek the counsel of a "true prophet" for clarifications. After doing all these, he will wait patiently for the unfolding of the will of God, and with thanksgiving, he will accept whatever comes his way. As Christians, we cannot claim to rely on God and, at the same time, lean on our knowledge or understanding. We cannot teach God what He should do though we may humbly make our requests known to Him. Therefore, we should stop approaching God with sentiments after failing in our quest to do things in our way.

Where Do We Go from Here?

With all said and done, we need to accept what has become an experience in spiritualism. When prophecy fails and it appears that the prophets have failed the people, they need to return to the drawing board. There is no point in reinterpreting the prophecy or shifting the date for the manifestation of the prophecy. Remember that many individuals failed in their prediction of the second coming of Christ when the Bible declared that the date is unknown even by angels. Prophets need to face the reality of having misled the public simply by playing gods. They need to reassess the situation and confront their followers with the truth. The basic principle is to understand where they have erred and take the necessary steps to correct their failures. Firstly, they need to confess their sins to God and seek His forgiveness. Following which, they need to seek the face of God for the wisdom and strength to move on. They need to go back to the Bible and rebuild their spiritual foundation. Then they need to work on restoring their followers' trust and teach them about the truth embedded in the Bible.

What Do We Hope to Achieve?

The Bible teaches us that "Jesus Christ is the Way, the Truth, and the Life" (John 14:6). Anything that has to do with the Messiah and His church has to be compatible with the truth of the Bible. Anything apart from the truth is not the truth, and the only way to do things right is to do it in the right way. When a situation like this occurs, we need to examine the incidence, whether it has to do with the truth and whether it conforms with the truth. If the incidence is not compatible with the truth, we need to address the fault. We will do this by putting the prophets and their allies (other members of the clergy) in a fault position, making them realize their mistake compared to the truth, and enabling and allowing them to take a new position compatible with the truth.

The next step is to meet with the congregation members and disabuse them of the fault through a re-education while emphasizing the truth of the subject. We should try to affirm the truth with the Bible and compare the fault with the fact that the Bible reveals. In doing this, we should try to bring them to a level of faith renewal that will rekindle hope in the church and the gospel message and renew a form of confidence in the leadership of the clergy. We should also try to reconcile members with opposing views if necessary. Finally, we need to expose our new opinion to the public because they are the field for the harvest that we will eventually visit with the gospel truth in the immediate and near future. By rightly informing the public, we are preparing the field for a future of bountiful harvest.

How Do We Begin?

When a prophet finds himself in a situation like this, understanding the problem will make it easier to find a way out of the unfortunate situation. With his understanding, he is to accept the fault as his own based on the truth of the matter and proceed to make amends. Firstly, the prophet needs to talk with the elders of his congregation, humbly explain what has happened, and let them know how he will inform the members about his failure. He should seek the opinion of the elders and gain their support. Secondly, the message should be communicated to group leaders that will, in turn, discuss the same with members of their groups. Finally, the prophet should mount the pulpit and give a message on the matter at hand, basing his explanations on a well-grounded Christology.

A prophecy that generates a broader level of controversy and attention will require a larger body like a Christian association or Christian leaders coming together to present a common front. This exercise will require intervention at both the general and local levels, but the larger body of believers should sponsor the conversation. The larger body should make a policy statement rooted in Christian love and ideals, followed by the local units breaking down the message to members of their local congregations. Where the church has been divided into opposing teams, efforts should be aimed at genuine Christian reconciliation and not at trading blames. The essence of Christian love transcends any controversy that may divide the church. The unity of the church is non-negotiable and cannot be exchanged for anything, and the earlier the church moves toward genuine reconciliation, the better the outcome.

In general, the way to address issues of this nature is to confront the truth, accept mistakes, and begin rebuilding relationships and rebuilding hope among members of the religious group. The clergy group must be rebuilt in preparation for the challenges ahead. The work of rebuilding the community of believers involves building trust and knowledge. Rebuilding the clergy group will involve individual and group therapies of admonishing one another as well as encouraging one another. Rebuilding the congregation will be preceded by rebuilding the relationship between the clergy and the community of believers. This arrangement is necessary because trust must be earned before any meaningful interaction can take place. After rebuilding trust, the clergy can now begin the work of building the trust, faith, and hope of believers about the purpose of the church.

The church urgently needs genuine reconciliation, but the best way to go about it is what I do not know though this book has offered a recommendation. The devil who tried to destroy the church will not relent on his aim, and the matter should not be swept under the carpet. Instead, the demons who turned prophets, pastors, and elders to debaters should be identified and destroyed. These are the politicians and the gullible Christians who I will refer to as the little foxes that spoil the vines (Song of Sol. 2:15). The politicians should be put in their rightful places, while the Christians need a re-orientation to rebuild their faith. The clergy community needs to reevaluate itself to identify where the problem emanated, leading to the application of an effective solution. The Christian community needs to take a proper inventory of its activities and ensure that they comply with the purposes and the roles of the church. A re-education is necessary for Christian leadership. This is necessary because the "bride of Christ" purchased at a costly price requires good and spirit-led leadership.

The church leadership needs to wake up to its responsibilities of providing proper education and direction to those being led. Good information management is equally essential so that the church can now speak with one well-informed voice even though members are free to form their opinions according to the levels of their orientation. The Bible counseled that the thief comes to steal, to kill, and to destroy (John 10:10A). The devil is unrelenting, and he will attempt to return for another assault on the church. A door of opportunity has been found, and the church must seal this opening. The devil will also try other means; therefore, the church must be on high alert, be concerned with issues of paramount importance to the church, and put on the "whole armor of God" (Eph. 6:11). Because the days are evil, the church must be sober and be vigilant at the same time. The church must be careful in dealing with carnal issues, bearing in mind what the Bible said in John 17:14 that we are in the world, but not of the world. May the good Lord continue to build His church.

Back to Our Root

The role of the church is to win souls into the kingdom of God, while the purpose of the church is to prepare Christians for eternal life just as they enjoy the reality and the benevolence of God in the present world. These two items should be paramount and openly displayed as the functions of the church. The knowledge of God is the essential ingredient for Christian growth. In contrast, the Christian life is the essence of this knowledge as Christians enjoy the kingdom of God on earth while preparing for eternity in heaven. The church must shun controversies but must be ready to do the work of evangelism. Members gained to the church through evangelism should be well-groomed to become vast in the knowledge of the Scriptures. They should be taught about Christian discipline and Christian love as they grow to become mature Christians. Different categories of trained teachers and instructors must be available for various groups of church members like the children, teens, adults, and the elderly. Church doctrines must be appropriately inculcated into the members, and methodically, they should be schooled about the reason for their faith. They must be brought to the understanding that Christian life is about happiness, peace, and joy of the Holy Ghost and not about eating and drinking and all that is attached to them. Christians should be made to understand the will of God and that God does not act outside of His sovereign will. They should realize that God's thought is different and higher than human thoughts and that every Christian must be ready to surrender to the will of God in all things. Christians should be thankful to God for everything, including when prayers are not answered according to their wishes despite the directive to always pray about everything. They should be advised to avoid unnecessary arguments and consistently apply the golden rule in these words attributed to (John Wesley and St. Augustine of Hippo) "In Essentials Unity, In Non-Essentials Liberty, In All Things Charity."

Focusing on the Bible

There is no way there will never be controversies or disagreements within a church. Discussions and debates about social and material issues are pardonable, but we must realize that as Christians, we are not of this world, even though we are in the world as living human beings. Individuals with different orientations and perceptions will have disagreements, but issues must be resolved amicably in love while respecting one another. Controversies that will pitch one group against another must be avoided because it will disturb the unity of the church that is essential for its spiritualism and survival. Therefore, the church must endeavor to create a Christian culture that will be handed over from one generation of worshippers to another. Ensuring a culture that endures is not achievable with written rules but by teaching a sound knowledge of church doctrines. Both written doctrines like sin, salvation, holiness, etc., and unwritten ones like Christian love, respect, and church unity, etc., should be taught during Bible studies so that individual members will know what is expected of them at every stage of their Christian growth.

Part VI

God Will Work Out His Plan

"I will build My Church, and the gates of hell shall not prevail against it." This verse in Mathew chapter 16 verse 18 is a promise of God concerning His church. There may be problems here and there, but the church will continue to thrive just like it has survived many tribulations over many centuries. As stated earlier in this book, God's purpose will always be fulfilled because of His sovereignty over the affairs of the world He created. The fallout of any unfortunate event will linger on as long as men remain in defiance of the plan of God. God's timing is different from man's timing. The Bible makes this explicitly clear that a day with the Lord is like a thousand years. Because God lives outside time, the timing of everything is within His control. Because humans live within the space of time, the situation being experienced by the church may be shortened or prolonged due to its submission or non-surrender to the will of God. The goodness of God can be extended if we remain obedient and devoted to God, while God's wrath may endure for a long time when we act stubbornly toward the purpose of God. Messengers of God should be aware of this fact and tailor their actions and teachings to reflect this divine truth.

God Is the Ultimate

To get a clear understanding of what is going on around us is to be heavenly focused. By this, I mean we should see God as the subject matter and every other thing as a situation that He allows to happen. Learning about God will help us understand God's character and attributes, His reason for creating us in His image, and His plan for our world. In many cases, humans tend to study the Word and try to make a god that fits into the subject of their imaginations. But learning about God as the source will help us understand what is going on in our world, the world that He created. Understanding this will give us a better perspective in understanding the goodness that we enjoy, the maladies that we made for ourselves, and the best way to live a peaceful life in harmony with God's laws. This is another fact that should be understood by our religious leaders first and then be inculcated into the minds of their followers. This way, they will be able to understand the truth and apply the same to their daily lives.

On a Personal Note

If there is one thing that I will advocate for all readers of this book, that thing will be the truth. I would employ everyone to search for the truth, find the truth, and hold on to this truth. But, unfortunately, we are often exposed to lies and half-truths daily. These lies and half-truths are responsible for misunderstandings among individuals and races. This falsehood and half-truths are also the foundation of all religious ideologies. Being part of this world, the church is not immune to these societal problems, especially when it has allowed itself to be used as a political tool. The church will become a political tool when the members lose hold of their calling and follow the way of the world. The church is always expected to realize that Christians are in the world but not of the world (John 17:14-16), and at the same time, the salt of the earth and the light of the world (Matt. 5:13-16). Whenever the church fails to realize this fact, it allows the world to enter and influence it instead of the church acting as the light of the world and illuminating it by its truth.

The conspiracy theories surrounding the COVID-19 pandemic have resulted in many unnecessary deaths and disabilities even within the church. These unnecessary sufferings were caused by conspiracy theorists with the aid of some Christians propagating the news that the pandemic is a farce and that vaccination is an attempt at colonizing the world by the Antichrist. Christians are expected to be wise (1 Peter 5:8). They are expected to search for the truth, confirm the truth, and hold on to the truth. The devilish infiltration of the church brought about the disorganization that was witnessed, and the world found it difficult to distinguish between the real and the unreal prophets. The result was that ministers shamefully and ignorantly pushed lies embedded in conspiracy theories, and thus Christendom became divided. In a sane society, it is the role of the church to seek the harmonization of spiritualism with science. The Christian of all souls is not expected to be ignorant.

The situation of the presidential prophesies and the COVID-19 conspiracies are seeds that have been sown into America, even into the church in America. According to the universal law of seedtime and the harvest, the seed of discord is expected to grow and produce fruits of more confusion. Whatever we do is both an action and a reaction, and the involvement of Christians in the controversy is a reaction to what is happening in the world around us. Unfortunately, the evil one succeeded in penetrating the church through the walls already broken within the church. The performers or the creators of the controversies are still around, and they are coming back for which the church must be prepared. A vital preparation by the church for the oncoming assault is to carefully explain the wrongs to members and engage in a proper debriefing to remove the effects of the assault from members and the church. A carefully planned education should follow based on the position of the church and what is expected of individual members. They equally should be reminded of the purpose of the church and their roles as members of the church.

The Presidential Prophecy

Americans judge their presidents according to their performances. For example, it is the tradition in American politics to label the president an antichrist, especially when the presidential policies contrast Christian expectations. In one instance, a former president of the United States was called the Antichrist probably because of his passion for members of other religious groups or his disdain for the adherents of another religion. Also, many former presidents have been called the Antichrist, but none of them have performed the roles ascribed to that personality in the Bible. Usually, there were presidential prophecies before every election, and not long ago, one of the candidates was predicted to be the chosen one instead of his co-contestant. The prophecy also claimed that he would act as president for two terms. Because of this prophecy, he was seen as the individual who would return America and Americans to God. This thought was conceived because of his sympathy for the demands from the adherents of the Christian faith.

The first part of the prophecy became a fulfillment, or should I say a happenstance? Only God knows, and only those who received the revelation can provide the answer to this question. The election was conducted, and the individual with the highest number of votes was declared the winner. However, throughout the presidency, the mark of Christianity was neither felt in the presidency nor the nation. Instead, the country witnessed chaos on every front. The man who God will use does not have to be a Christian, nor does he have to be of another religion. Instead, he will be a person purposefully chosen by God for a specific assignment. The favorite of the Christian electorates could not contribute to love and harmony within the Christian community, but what was witnessed was division in the church that was an extension of the disunity witnessed throughout the nation. The regime later earned the rebuke of some Christians, and the presidency lost the support of some toward the end of the tenure.

Midway into the administration of the presidency, we witnessed a severe division of Americans who refused to unite after the presidential election due to the tense state of the political environment. We saw a shift from the majority support of members of the president's party while the support from the Christians began to wane. However, the presidency succeeded in some actions that pacified the Christian community, but it was not enough to convince the community of believers. Finally, the election was conducted, but the incumbent lost the presidential election, and the presidency could not serve the second term as predicted. The presidency and its supporters rejected the election results on the premise that the election was rigged against their party.

The second part of the prophecy concerned with the second term appears to be in jeopardy. The prophesied candidate lost the election, and another politician was sworn in as the new president of the United States of America. If the prophecy was false, that appears to be the end to the prophecy. If the prophecy was right and true, that means we need to return to the drawing board to find out the best way to interpret the prophecy. A true prophecy will surely come to pass, even though it may take a long time. The common problem we have as humans could be with the interpretation of the prophecy, the timing of the prophecy, or the expected method or form that the manifestation of the prophecy will take.

Relationship of the Prophecy with the Present Situation

As believers and readers of prophecy, the question that should come to our minds is what happened to the prophecy concerning the second term and the proclaimed mission of the former president to return America to God, especially now that he lost the presidential election. I think the hope of regaining the winnings of the last election has been lost when every legal battle contested at changing the election commission's decision has been lost. The efforts of his supporters as they tried to disrupt the certification process were also unsuccessful. Also, the final hope was dashed when Congress approved the election results. The best way to answer these questions is to relate the prophecy to the present situation in the country. Performing a re-assessment of the whole situation is necessary because God will always do what He promised. The problem with human beings is that the issue of fake prophecies and wrong interpretation of prophecy rests in the domain of men.

The plan of God to return America to Himself is not in doubt because He does not want anyone to perish (2 Peter 3:9B). As explained earlier in this book, prophecy occurs when there is a problem in the land, and God's children are full of expectations for answers to their fervent prayers. Prophecy also happens when God wants to move in His usual way and thus announce His plan to His prophets. The issue of the second term can also be seen from a different dimension. For example, it may be that the former president is coming back again through another election or that the effect or influence of his single term will endure throughout the present regime. The reality of the former explanation is feasible if the ex-president can muster enough courage to contest the next election by gaining the approval of his political party and winning enough support from the populace. The other party may also clear the way for him if the incumbent performs woefully to the extent that most Americans prefer the former president's return to the White House.

The plan of God for America will surely come to pass whether Americans like it or not. A seed has been sown that will germinate and bear fruit for every action that a man takes, whether good or bad. The effects of actions taken by our leaders in the past are responsible for what we are experiencing today, and the actions by the architects in the previous regime are the foundation for what we are about to experience. The division witnessed as a fallout of the election may be child's play to what will be experienced. The sympathizers of the previous administration will still support other issues on the agenda of the last regime. The effects are unfolding, and all we need to do is open our eyes to witness the direction that the country is heading. A Christian is expected to live the Christian life and perform his duties to his country. One of the duties of a Christian is to pray for those in authority so that the peace of God shall continue to reign in the land. We should also pray for righteousness to reign in the land because peace and prosperity without righteousness is a problem waiting to happen. No matter our personal bias, we owe a duty as Christians to pray for the will of God to prevail in the land. How God executes His will should not be our concern.

A Biblical Example

The idea of two individuals ruling in the affairs of a nation is not new. Just as the Almighty God is ruling over the affairs of His creation, the devil also is ruling in the hearts of those people who he has captured to do his will (2 Tim. 2:26). This statement is a spiritual fact. According to historical records, there are incidences of more than one individual having rulership over the people of Israel in biblical times. Co-regency is the term used to describe this phenomenon in the Bible, and it occurred when two individuals were recorded ruling in Israel at the same

God Will Work Out His Plan

time. Also, examples abound in the Bible where a father and his son reigned together simultaneously. The first example was the reign of Hezekiah and Manasseh, as recorded in 2 Kings chapters 18-20 and 2 Kings 21:1-18. The same story was confirmed in 2 Chronicles 32:33 and 2 Chronicles 33:1. According to historians, Hezekiah reigned from 715 BC to 686 BC, while his son Manasseh reigned from 697 BC to 642 BC. The second example was the reigns of King David and Solomon, his son, where Solomon's coronation took place at the father's insistence (1 Kings 1:28-40).

Yet another form of co-regency occurred in the Bible, and this one is amusing. While Saul was ruling as king over Israel, David was anointed to become king of Israel, in place of King Saul, who had been rejected by God (1 Sam. 16:13). David was anointed the second time to be king of Judah by the men of Judah (2 Sam. 2:4). Again, David was anointed the third time to be accepted as king of Israel by the elders of Israel (2 Sam. 5:3). In summary, David was anointed three times before he became the king, and during this period, Saul was still reigning over the affairs of the nation of Israel. The main point here is that some Israelites remained loyal to King Saul while King David also enjoyed the loyalty of his admirers. The implication of co-regency to the American situation is that the physical reign of the former president may be over. Still, the effect of his rule and his influence over America may linger on for some time. It is important to note that all Americans do not accept the current president, and the group that is not loyal to him is ready to perform acts that may undermine his administration.

Relationship of the Prophesy to End Time Events

Kingdom comes, and kingdom goes. Many empires recorded in the Bible have become extinct, while many strong empires of the present day have been subdued. The reigning world power is the United States, and it appears that another country may soon become the next world power. A country like China or Russia or an amalgamation of some countries like China and Russia should be on our watch list. There is no doubt that God loves the United States of America, but He hates seeing America becoming a sinful nation. Prosperity has been known to drive people away from God, but a lack of it brings people down to their knees. If God wants to save this country, just like I believe He has planned to, He will first remove His comfort that diverts the people's attention from Him and create a thirst for His intervention.

God is known as a comforter to the afflicted, and He equally afflicts the comfortable who are lawless. The church needs to awake from slumber before God decides to visit us, just like He did to the land of Sodom and Gomorrah. Christians should embark on mass evangelism to bring the nation back to God to avert this discomfiture. The neglect of this may result in the removal of prosperity and the imposition of hardship that will drive people back to God, and this thirst for God will create the much-awaited revival that will wake Americans up from slumber. The implication of this is that all believers must be prepared for the days ahead. The preparation will have two foci. One is to prepare for an economic recession by saving for the rainy day. The second one is to prepare for large-scale evangelism that will sweep across the country.

A Word for Christian Leaders

Prophecy is a controversial doctrine, and care must be taken when handling the subject. Always, there are forms of emotional sensationalism whenever the issue of prophecy is being discussed. And this emotional involvement may affect the reception and interpretation of prophecy. Prophets are therefore ethically bound to understand their art in accordance with their calling and with absolute submission to the will of God so that they can render their service without favor or partiality. Sound knowledge of the subject is essential if the prophet will enjoy a career that endures. He must exercise caution when dealing with desperate individuals for solutions that he cannot give while offering to tell them only what God has approved. Christian leaders occupy an exalted position in society, and they should be wary of their roles in political matters. They should be seen as individuals who teach the truth only, expose wrongs, and guide members of the public in deciding on what to do with the truth. However, care must be taken so that they do not impose their opinion on their followers.

Christian leaders should see themselves as the conscience of the society and must be ready to defend the truth and the defenseless members of the society. As the conscience of the nation, Christian leaders should play the role of nation-builders by building bridges between different communities of people and advocating for good government and citizenship. They should be ready to play the role of umpires whenever a problem arises and be prepared to confront and condemn every appearance of evil. They should be able to read the mind of the society and be ready to protect members of their delegation from the societal influence that may likely injury the corporate existence of the church. They should try not to be involved in unnecessary arguments but should listen actively and devise ways to resolve issues amicably without destroying the corporate love that binds the church together.

They should be ready to resolve conflicts among members whenever things go wrong. In this way, they will be setting an excellent example for their membership and society. They should never forget that their lifestyle is the only epistle that society reads. Living a life of holiness with a flair for evangelism will help portray the church as a peace-loving institution and the clergy as a noble calling. When there is peace in the church, it becomes a ready place of abode for those experiencing turmoil. The goodness of the church can be showcased at times of evangelism, and those who have been destined to enter the kingdom of the Son will willingly be wooed into the fold of the church. Christians need to evangelize with their words, but they will win more souls if their living style is worthy of emulation.

At a time of national turmoil, the clergy must be ready to offer a form of sympathetic understanding and make the church a place of succor to the populace, especially members of their congregation. While anticipating the future, they should be able to make projections out of the present situation and prayerfully submit the outcome to the will of God. They should carry members of their congregation along with this thought, beginning with the elders while explaining the spiritual implication of the situation and offering advice to them, and at the same time suing for peace. In playing this role, they should remember never to allow the Christian community to be used as a launching pad for controversial debates or conspiracy theories that may damage the community's cohesion. The first obligation of the clergy is to the church, and they must strive to keep the church in good health, and this health is what should be projected to society at large.

The Conclusion

The author has explored the church and its role in society and examined the issue of church leadership, emphasizing the prophetic ministry. He also discussed the relationship between Christian leadership and the importance of a well-developed biblical worldview that indicates Christian maturity. The message in this book is three-fold. The first one is to enlighten the seekers of prophecy and empower them to make an informed and objective decision concerning prophecies that affect their lives. After reviewing this book in relation to the events of the presidential prophecy and the COVID-19 conspiracy, every consumer of prophecy or follower of prophets should have a rethink on the way they react to messages they hear and also be mindful of the outcome of their reaction as it affects their neighbors and the nation as a whole.

The second one is for prophets and other church leaders to be reminded of the sacredness of their calling and make conscious efforts to sanitize the church and protect believers and the general public from the harmful effects of fake prophecy. The outcome of the events witnessed is a call for caution in their utterances and how they manage their messages because the public's reaction to their messages is unpredictable. And the effects of the public response to their messages cannot be predicted. As Christians, it is apparent that we cannot fully

Politics, Prophesy, and The Pillage of the Church

understand the meaning of some prophecies. But we have the Holy Spirit Who can reveal a prophecy and provide the interpretation. It is a waste of time to create arguments over the meaning, interpretation, or manifestation of prophecies. So why do we create a controversy over God's sovereign will when the depth of His knowledge is unfathomable? Why do we have to create arguments in the church to the extent of breaching the peaceful coexistence of members? Because prophecy is a spiritual phenomenon that can only be spiritually discerned, we ought not to build our lives on prophecy but instead rely upon prophecy as our guide.

The third and final part of the message is for the church to garner its energy and resources toward evangelizing the lost and building up the converts. The converts that are not built up will be a burden to the church or soon find their ways back to the world, while controversies in the Christian circle will repel newly converted ones from the church. We can conclude that prophecy is God's gift to the church. If properly harnessed, it will be beneficial to the church and the society, particularly in dealing with the moment and preparing for the future. In this way, the present church can be preserved, while the future of the church can be guaranteed. Failure to protect the church now and in the future will continue to expose the church to different ideologies that will seriously jeopardize the fundamental functions and roles of the church. As Christians, we owe it a divine duty to take proactive measures that will preserve the sanity of the church until the return of the Master. "When the Son of Man comes, will He find faith on earth?" (Luke 18:8B).

www.ingramcontent.com/pod-product-compliance
Ingram Content Group UK Ltd.
Pitfield, Milton Keynes, MK11 3LW, UK
UKHW041950230426
12048UKWH00008B/240

**Poets and the
Algerian War**